People and machines

How Things Work tells you about the things that people use at work, at home and at play. It takes things from everyday life and explains how each of them works. It also tells you what goes on behind the scenes in shops and offices, and in the life of a city. The book shows you that many of the things you see around you are made by people.

Making life easier
People have always made tools to help them survive. Early people cut and carved wood to make spears to kill animals for food. Today, most people do not hunt for food, but work to earn the money to buy it at a shop. To make their work easier, people often use **machines**.

People working together
Today's work is often complicated. It takes many people working in an organized way to get the job done. Sometimes workers compete to prove they are the best. Other times they work together to reach a goal.

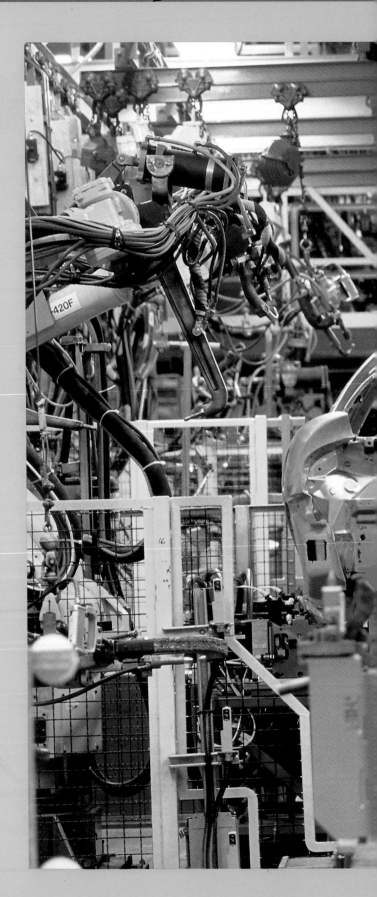

Machines people use
Whether it's an electronic calculator or cash register, a delivery truck or a fork-lift truck, people use machines to make work easier. In factories, people even use machines to make other machines.

Machines and movement

There are many different kinds of **machine**.
Machines can be simple, like screwdrivers,
or complicated, like cars. Complicated machines
have hundreds of parts that work together to do a job.

Machines and energy

Just like people, machines need **energy**
to do work. This energy
can come from
many **sources**.

Machines can be
powered by **fuels**
(say "fyoo-els")
such as oil and
coal, electrical
generators (say
"jen-er-ay-tors"),
nuclear energy,
batteries, the
Sun, or even
by people's
muscles.

Forces

When machines are given energy, they begin to work. In order to do a job, machines change natural **forces** in some way. A screwdriver changes a small force from a hand into a large force that can turn a screw in wood. A car changes the force from moving parts inside the engine into the force that drives the wheels round.

▲ A digger uses electricity to create a **powerful** force that can lift heavy loads.

Aeroplane

An aeroplane is a flying **machine** with wings and engines. It is used to carry goods or people over long distances. The smallest planes seat only one or two people, but huge passenger planes can carry more than 400 people on board. These large planes usually have a crew with a pilot, co-pilot and flight attendants who look after the passengers.

How a plane flies

Planes can fly because they have wings. If you look at a plane from the side, you will see that the wings have a curved shape. It is this shape that lifts the plane off the ground.

The **streamlined** shape of the aeroplane allows air to flow past the plane smoothly so that it can fly faster.

aeroplane rising

air flowing over wing

At take-off, air rushing over the wings creates a **force** called lift. The air below the wings pushes the plane up so that it flies.

Flying is the quickest way to travel. Planes are so fast that on the same day you can have breakfast in London and dinner in New York! Yet travelling by plane is still quite new. The first passenger planes flew not long before your grandparents were born.

Jet engines

Large modern planes are powered by jet engines that burn **fuel** (say "fyoo-el"). The engines suck in air at the front and then blast it out at the back. The plane shoots forward like a balloon when someone lets the air inside it escape.

Although planes look heavy, the **materials** (say "ma-tir-ee-als") they are made of, such as aluminium, are light. They stay up in the air because, when they are travelling fast, the lift pushing them up is greater than the weight pulling them down.

▼ Aeroplanes used in snowy places have skis fitted to their wheels for landing.

▲ The aluminium Lockheed F-117A "Stealth" bomber is covered with a special paint so that it cannot be picked up by **radar**.

At the airport
Each time a plane lands, it is prepared for its next flight by different groups of people. The ground crew makes sure the plane has enough fuel. **Engineers** check many of the plane's electronic control systems. Cleaners clean the passenger cabin and remove the rubbish. The kitchen staff load food and drinks on to the aeroplane.

▲ Cargo is loaded onto a Boeing 747 through its nose. The plane's fuel tank has to carry over 170,000 litres of fuel.

13

Bathroom

The bathroom is where you keep yourself clean. It has a basin, a bath or shower, and usually has a toilet. Keeping clean is important for good health. Regular washing gets rid of the invisible **germs** on your body that can make you smell bad and become sick.

Water and plumbing
Water is usually pumped into homes from the local water system or an underground well. Some water travels along narrow, hidden pipes to a tank to be heated up before it is used. Cold water goes by pipe straight to the kitchen or bathroom. Dirty water goes from the house into underground pipes called sewers. From there it is taken away to be cleaned at a sewage **treatment plant**.

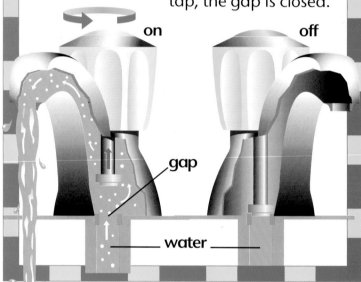

Inside a tap

When you turn on a tap, you open a gap which allows the water in the pipe to flow through. When you turn off the tap, the gap is closed.

on   off

gap

water

Water on the move

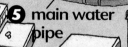

4 storage tower

6 home

5 main water pipe

2 pumping station

1 river

3 treatment plant

now picture this

If you lined up end-to-end all the water pipes used in a two-bedroom flat, they would be nearly as long as 10 railway wagons.

A good flush

As the toilet flushes, clean water pushes the dirty water out. Water in the bottom of the toilet keeps out bad smells from the sewers.

Why use shampoo?

The dirt in your hair is greasy and can't be washed out by water alone. A gentle detergent called shampoo loosens the grease, so that you can rinse it away with clean water.

▶ Soap and bubble bath clean your skin in the same way that shampoo cleans your hair.

7 sewer

8 sewage treatment plant

10 sea

9 clean water

Bike

▶ A few racing bikes have solid wheels made of carbon fibre. These wheels are very lightweight.

A bike is a two-wheeled **vehicle** (say "vee-ick-el") that both children and adults can ride. Most bikes have no engine. Their **energy** comes from you, as you push the pedals with your feet. Learning to balance on a bike is tricky at first, but it gets easier. When a bike is moving fast, it stops wobbling. This is because the **force** moving the bike forward is stronger than the force pulling the bike down. Once you have learned how to ride a bike, you never forget how it is done.

Bike parts

The gears give the bike greater force when you cycle uphill. To work properly, the gears need to be oiled regularly.

ALWAYS WEAR A BICYCLE HELMET TO PROTECT YOUR HEAD IF YOU FALL. MAKE SURE YOU WEAR LIGHT CLOTHES THAT CAN BE EASILY SEEN, ESPECIALLY WHEN CYCLING AT NIGHT.

The bike pump pushes air into the tyres to give a more comfortable ride.

The chain carries the force from the pedals to the back wheel and makes it turn. It should be well oiled to keep it moving smoothly.

The metal spokes make the wheels strong, but light.

now picture this

Take a bike

Bikes are a very **efficient** (say "e-fish-ent") form of transport. They don't need petrol or expensive repairs. They are easy to park and are never held up in traffic jams. Best of all, they have no **fumes** to pollute the **environment**.

The longest bike ever built had seats for 35 riders and was over 20 metres long.

The handlebars are for steering.

▲ Bikes are cheap and easy to run. In many countries, bicycles are used as family cars.

The brakes rub against the wheels to slow them down and make them stop. They should be kept clean so that they can grip the tyres properly.

The tyres have a pattern on them called the tread. This helps the tyre grip the road when it's wet.

17

Boat

A boat is a **vehicle** (say "vee-ick-el") that travels on water. Small boats are used to carry people over rivers and lakes, and along a coast. Larger boats, or ships, cross seas and oceans, but they work in much the same way.

Sink or swim?

Anything will float if it is lighter than water. As long as a boat isn't too heavy for its size, the push of the water upwards and inwards against it will keep the boat balanced and floating on the water's surface.

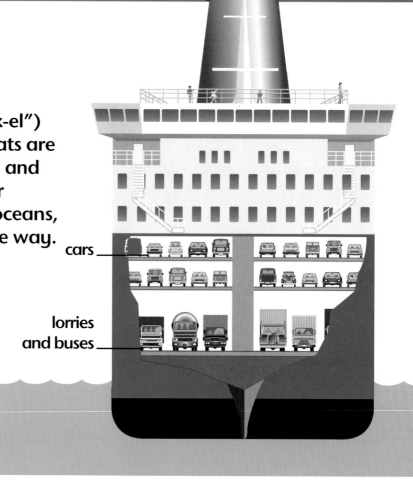

cars

lorries and buses

▲ Vehicles are carefully loaded onto a ferry. Heavy lorries are put low down in the ship to keep the ferry steady in strong winds.

◄ A raft is one of the simplest kinds of boat. It is made of logs that are tied together with rope.

Some oil tankers are more than 400 metres long. The sailors on them use bikes to get from one end of the deck to the other.

now picture this

Boats in motion

Boats use different kinds of **energy** to move.

Sailing boats are driven by the wind. Sometimes there is either too much of it or none at all!

Rowing boats have oars to move them through the water. The oars get their **force** from people's muscles, which get tired on long journeys.

Many boats have engines that turn a **propeller**. If they have enough **fuel** (say "fyoo-el"), they can travel far without relying on the wind.

▶ Modern ships are built by joining huge pieces of steel together on a framework.

Some boats are made of light **materials** (say "ma-tir-ee-als"), such as reeds, **fibreglass**, or aluminium. But modern ships aren't light in weight. They are huge, and made of heavy metals, such as steel. They stay afloat because of their big, hollow shape. Ships contain so much air that, even though they are so large, they are still lighter than water.

Book

A book is a way of presenting stories, information and pictures. It contains words printed or written on pages of paper, which are **bound** together in a cover. Different books tell you about different subjects. In a storybook, pictures often help to tell the story. Some books are so popular that they are printed in many different languages.

▲ This book has been printed in Greek, Spanish and English. Only the words have been changed.

Books are produced by publishers. A lot of people work together at the publishers to make a book. Each person has a different job.

The designer (say "de-zy-ner") decides how the book will look.

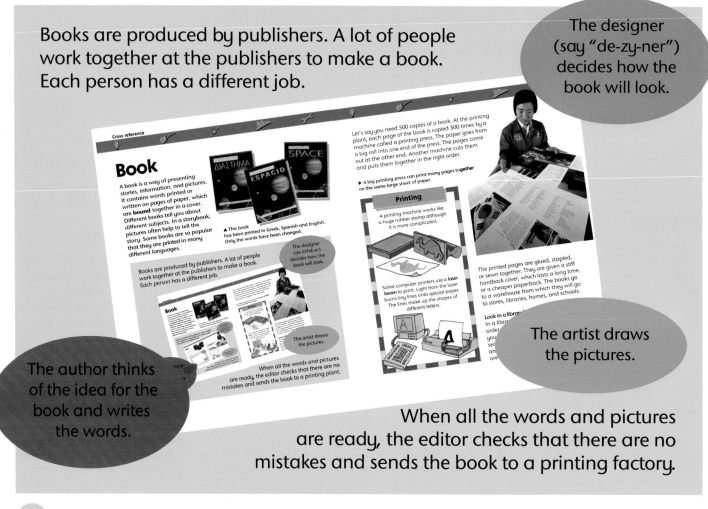

The artist draws the pictures.

The author thinks of the idea for the book and writes the words.

When all the words and pictures are ready, the editor checks that there are no mistakes and sends the book to a printing factory.

Making books

At a printing factory, each page of the book is copied hundreds and thousands of times by a machine called a printing press. The paper goes from a big roll into one end of the press and the pages come out at the other end. Another machine cuts them and puts them together in the right order.

▶ **A big printing press can print many pages together on the same large sheet of paper.**

Printing

Modern printing machines are huge and complicated but a rubber stamp works in the same way.

Some computer printers use a **laser beam** to print. Light from the laser burns tiny lines onto special paper. The lines make up the shapes of different letters.

The printed pages are glued, stapled or sewn together. They are given a stiff hardback cover, which lasts a long time, or a cheaper paper cover. The books go to a warehouse and then to shops, libraries, homes and schools.

Look in a library

In a library, books are kept in a special order, so that you can find the titles you want. Storybooks are kept in the fiction section. Fact books like this encyclopedia (say "en-sy-clo-pee-dee-a"), are kept in the non-fiction section.

Bridge

A bridge helps people, cars, lorries and bikes cross over a place where roads and paths can't normally go. There are bridges across rivers and valleys, streets and railways. On busy main roads, bridges called flyovers are built above junctions. These bridges help to keep **vehicles** (say "vee-ick-els") moving.

The longest suspension bridge in the world crosses the River Humber in England. It can support 170 big trucks.

now picture this

Bridge shapes

There are different kinds of bridge:

A flat board across a stream is a beam bridge. It's easy to build, but it isn't strong enough to hold much weight.

An arched bridge can hold up heavier weights. A row of arches joined together makes a strong bridge called a viaduct.

A suspension bridge also carries heavy loads, but across wider spaces. Thick cables, fixed to high towers at each end, hold the bridge up. Very strong winds can make a suspension bridge swing and sometimes even break.

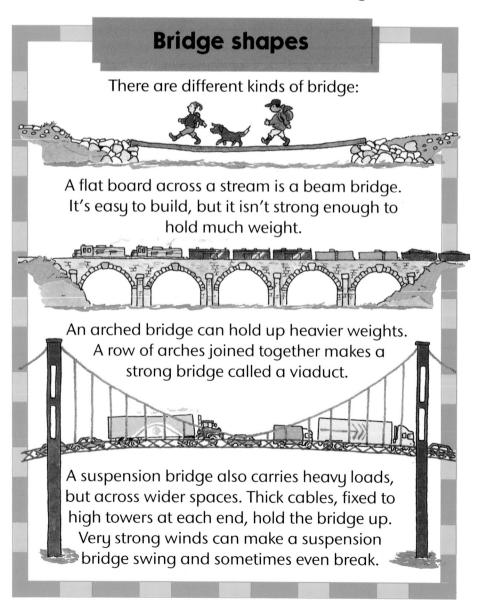

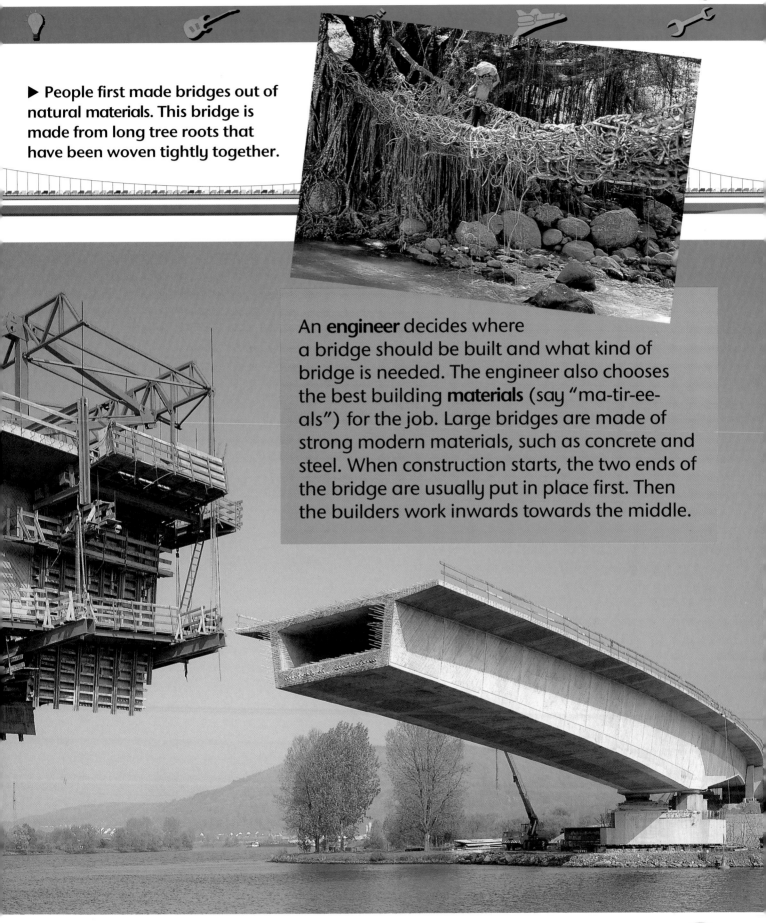

▶ People first made bridges out of natural materials. This bridge is made from long tree roots that have been woven tightly together.

An **engineer** decides where a bridge should be built and what kind of bridge is needed. The engineer also chooses the best building **materials** (say "ma-tir-ee-als") for the job. Large bridges are made of strong modern materials, such as concrete and steel. When construction starts, the two ends of the bridge are usually put in place first. Then the builders work inwards towards the middle.

Building

A building is a structure with strong walls and a roof. Schools, houses, offices, shops and factories are all buildings. A building can be a small room or a huge skyscraper. It takes many different people to build a new building, but they don't all work together. Instead they carry out their different jobs in stages.

A new house

1 The architect (say "ark-i-tekt") draws up plans of the new house, which the builders will follow.

2 A dump truck brings to the building site the small stones, cement and sand that are used to make concrete.

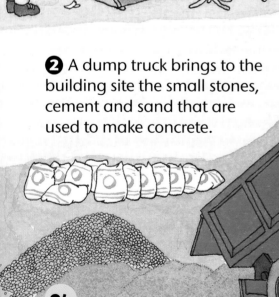

4 Builders use diggers to dig trenches for the foundations, which stop the building sinking. They fill the trenches with concrete.

3 Trenches are dug for the gas and water pipes, and for electricity cables.

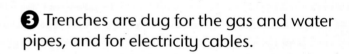

5 A cement mixer makes the cement used for building walls.

6 Bricklayers build the walls out of bricks or stone blocks cemented together.

7 Carpenters make the roof frame, lay floorboards, and fit the door and window frames.

8 Builders use scaffolding to reach high-up parts of the house.

9 Electricians fit electric wires and cables.

10 Plumbers fit water pipes in bathrooms and the kitchen. They also install pipes for the central heating.

11 Plasterers smooth the walls with plaster.

Bus

A bus is a large road **vehicle** (say "vee-ick-el") with a **powerful** engine and seats for passengers. Buses carry people around cities and towns, into cities from the countryside or from one city to another. They are a good, cheap way to get around, especially for people who don't have a car, and live far from a railway or underground line. Buses carry lots of people all at once, and help to keep the roads clear.

▲ Many people use trams or buses to travel to work in busy cities. Some trams and buses have two decks to carry more people.

A city bus

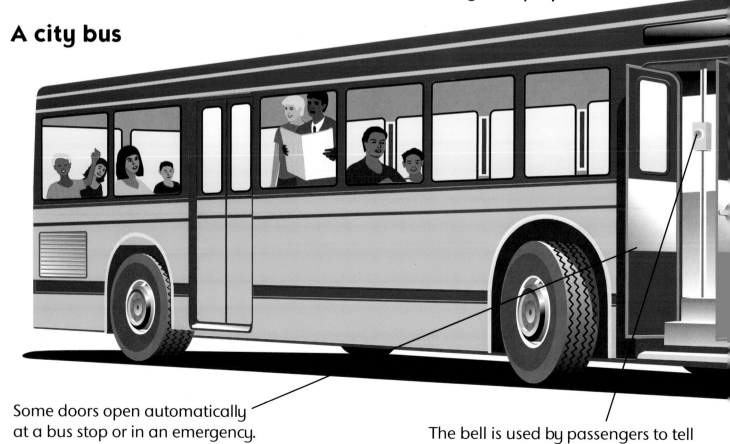

Some doors open automatically at a bus stop or in an emergency. Others are controlled by the driver.

The bell is used by passengers to tell the driver to stop at the next stop.

Catching a bus

Buses run to every district of a city. Passengers find out when their bus runs from a timetable. They wait at the bus stop for the bus and when it arrives they pay a fare to travel on it.

The radio allows the driver to keep in touch with the bus company head office.

▲ **In poorer countries** buses are often the only way people can travel to market, unless they walk.

In countries that do not have many cars or fast roads, buses are very important. In the wet season, buses can be the only vehicles able to travel along muddy roads to far-away villages. If there are not enough buses, old trucks or vans may be used to carry people as well.

The ticket machine prints tickets that show the fare a passenger has paid.

Trams

Some places have trams instead of buses. Trams run on electricity picked up from cables running high above the street by a long metal arm on their roof.

Camera

A camera is a **machine** that is used to take photographs. The first cameras appeared in the 1830s. The most common kind of modern camera can be carried in your hand and takes photographs that are printed onto paper. Other cameras, such as video and movie cameras, take moving pictures that you watch on a television or at a cinema.

▶ To keep the camera steady while taking a photograph, photographers fix the camera to a stand called a tripod.

Taking a photograph

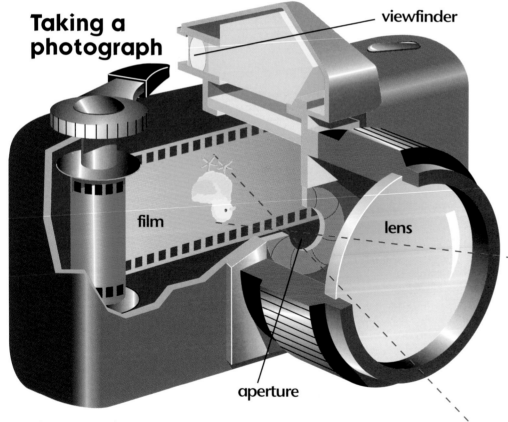

viewfinder

film

lens

aperture

❸ Where the coating of the film is hit by light, it makes a picture.

❶ The viewfinder shows the picture you are about to take.

❷ When you press the button, a hole called the aperture (say "ap-ert-your") opens in the camera front. Light passing through the **lens** is directed through the aperture onto the film.

Using photographs

People take photographs for different reasons. Family photos help people to remember places that they've visited and the people they've known. Photographs used in newspapers and magazines are not only interesting, but may be better than words at explaining what has happened. Photographs help people to find out what life was like in the past, or during an event such as a war.

Did you know?

Your brain can see only 10 single pictures every second. After this the pictures begin to join together.

The world's fastest camera takes 33,000 million pictures every second. It belongs to the Imperial College of Science and Technology in London.

The world's largest negative was made in America in 1992. It is seven metres long.

4 At a laboratory (say "lab-o-ra-tree"), parts of the film coating without pictures are washed off. A special bath "fixes" the pictures on the film in a strip of **negatives**.

▲ Underwater cameras have helped scientists to discover much more about life in the ocean.

— film

photograph

negative

5 When light is shone through a negative onto special paper, a photograph is made. One negative can make hundreds of pictures.

Moving pictures

Movie cameras take pictures that seem to move. In fact they take many still pictures every second. Your brain "sees" each picture for a while after it has disappeared. When the pictures are shown quickly one after another, they overlap and seem to join together in a moving scene.

Car

A car is a road **vehicle** (say "vee-ick-el") with four wheels and an engine. It is the most popular kind of transport in the world. If you travel by car you don't have to keep to a timetable or follow bus routes or railways. Cars have plenty of room for passengers as well as their luggage.

A family car

The steering wheel turns the front wheels.

The ignition key turns and creates sparks that set off explosions in the engine and make the car move.

Inside the engine

Cars usually get the **energy** to move from burning petrol inside their engines. As the petrol explodes, the **force** of the explosions makes parts of the engine move. As these parts move, they make the wheels turn.

The gears give the car the right amount of **power** to start moving or climb steep hills.

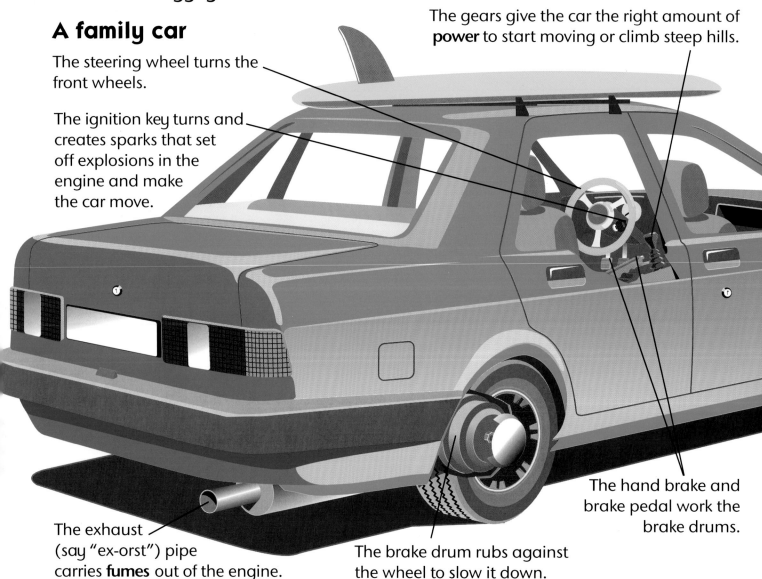

The hand brake and brake pedal work the brake drums.

The brake drum rubs against the wheel to slow it down.

The exhaust (say "ex-orst") pipe carries **fumes** out of the engine.

▲ During a race, the team of mechanics has to refuel a racing car and change its tyres in a few seconds.

Cars old and new

Car fumes are dirty and smelly and pollute the air. **Engineers** have made **filters** to try to solve this problem. A filter is put inside the car's exhaust pipe. The filters clean the dirty fumes as they pass into the air.

Modern cars can go twice as far as old cars on the same amount of petrol. Some are smaller than old cars and weigh much less. A few modern cars do not burn petrol, but use energy from the Sun and other **sources**.

Indicator lights warn other drivers that the car is going to turn left or right.

Headlights light up the road for driving at night.

▼ Cars that run on electricity are clean and quiet.

A car to suit you

Engineers design (say "de-zyne") cars for different uses. Racing cars are **streamlined** and very fast, but only have room for the driver. Family cars are slower than racing cars, but they have plenty of room for passengers and don't use as much petrol. An off-road vehicle is very powerful. Its big tyres can cope with the roughest tracks.

City

A city is a large area where thousands or millions of people live and work. To cope with such numbers of people, cities need excellent services. For example, they need plenty of electricity and water, and lots of schools for the children. City life is often fast and noisy, but there are lots of interesting things to do.

A modern city

1881

Restaurants in the city centre serve people dishes from all over the world.

The city centre may still have some old buildings from when the city was a town.

Drains carry water into the sewers.

Gas pipes carry gas into homes and offices for cooking and heating.

Underground systems allow people to cross the city quickly.

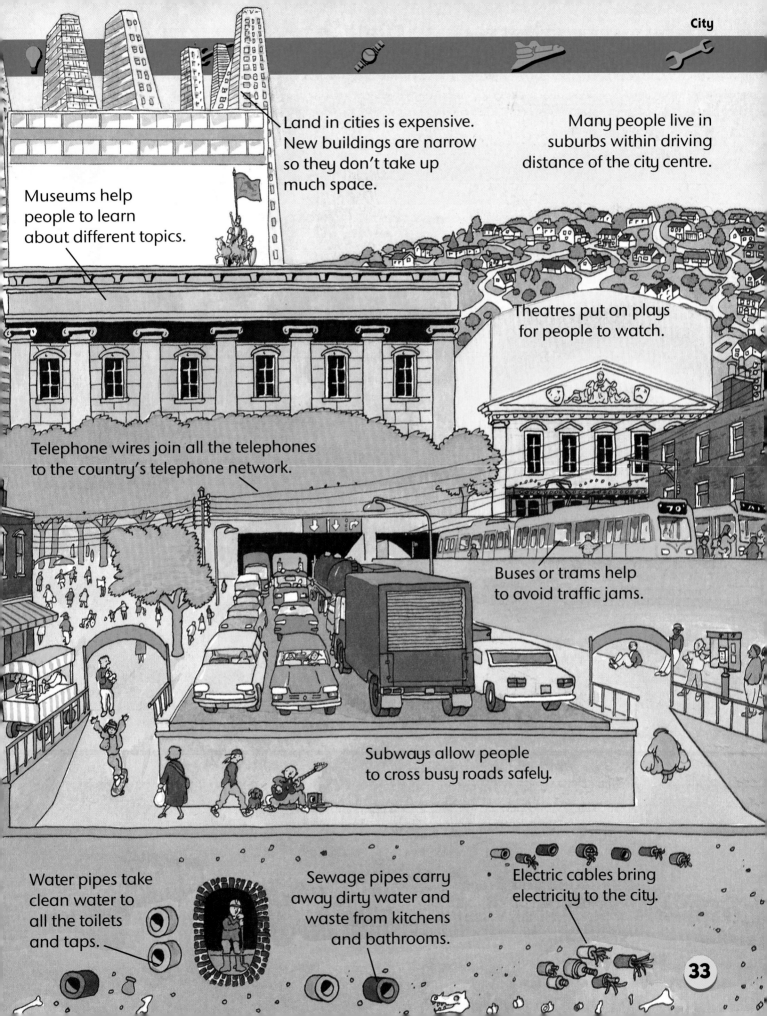

Land in cities is expensive. New buildings are narrow so they don't take up much space.

Many people live in suburbs within driving distance of the city centre.

Museums help people to learn about different topics.

Theatres put on plays for people to watch.

Telephone wires join all the telephones to the country's telephone network.

Buses or trams help to avoid traffic jams.

Subways allow people to cross busy roads safely.

Water pipes take clean water to all the toilets and taps.

Sewage pipes carry away dirty water and waste from kitchens and bathrooms.

Electric cables bring electricity to the city.

33

Clock

A clock measures the passing of time, and tells us what time it is. Some clocks tell the time with two hands that move around a numbered clock face. Digital clocks tell the time with numbers. They are often found on ovens or video **machines**. We use clocks all day long to help us arrive on time at school, to see a film or to meet a friend.

Time around the world

Only half of the Earth faces the Sun at a single time. When it is midday in one part of the world it is the middle of the night in another. The world is divided up into different time zones, so that all clocks read 12 o'clock when the Sun is highest in the sky, wherever the clock is.

Did you know?

Many modern watches will work under water. The latest diving watches will work in depths of up to 1,000 metres.

The most accurate clock in the world was made in California in 1991. It will lose only one second in 1.7 million years and costs £36,000 to buy.

Before 1687, clocks only had an hour hand.

▼ These clocks show the time in different parts of the world when it is midday in New York, USA.

9 am (same day)
Los Angeles, USA

5 pm (same day)
London, England

10 pm (same day)
Calcutta, India

Clocks with a difference

Hourglasses were invented hundreds of years ago. They used the flow of sand from one half of the glass to the other to measure the passing of time. It took one hour for all the sand to fall through to the other side of the hourglass.

An egg timer works like an hourglass, but it takes just three or four minutes for the sand to run through the timer. It's a handy way of knowing when your egg is boiled.

▶ The Ancient Romans used letters to represent numbers. Some clocks still use Roman numerals to tell the time.

2 am (next day)
Tokyo, Japan

Computer

A computer is a **machine** that works like an electronic brain. It stores much more infomation than most people's brains can, and sorts through it more quickly. However, a computer cannot work by itself. It has to be given instructions to tell it how to do even the simplest job.

A personal computer

Personal computers are small computers that are made for one person to use. Personal computers are found in many offices and schools.

◄ Some computers have a hand control, called a scanner, that can read maps. The computer copies the map onto its screen, ready to be used.

The keyboard is like a typewriter. Typing on it feeds information into the computer.

The information in the computer appears on the screen.

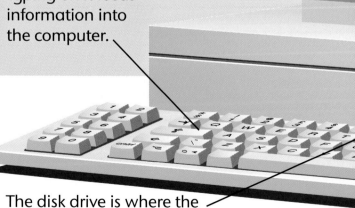

The disk drive is where the computer "reads" information off floppy disks.

Hardware and software

The screen, keyboard and disk drive of a computer are called computer hardware. The instructions that tell a computer to play a game or write a letter are called the program. Another name for the program is software.

Some computer uses

Engineers use computers when they design (say "de-zyne") new cars. An engineer can make small changes to the design and test them out on the computer screen, without having to build a different model each time.

The police use computers to compare one set of fingerprints with the many thousands of prints they have stored. A computer will find the matching set, if it's there, in just a matter of minutes. Then the police will know who has been at the scene of a crime.

Inside the computer is the hard disk. This is where information is stored and where all the instructions are carried out.

The printer prints information from the computer onto sheets of paper.

The mouse is a small hand control which moves an arrow on the screen.

Information can be stored on a floppy disk. Disks can be carried around and used in different computers.

37

Electricity

Electricity is a way of moving **energy** around. You can't see electricity, but you can see what it does. It gives us light and heat whenever we want, and it makes **machines** work. Electricity moves. A lightning flash in the sky is really electricity travelling between clouds and the ground. Electricity is powerful but can also be very dangerous, so we use it with care.

Electricity on the move

❶ Electricity is made in large **power stations**. Most power stations use coal, oil, or gas as **fuel** (say "fyoo-el") to heat water. Steam from the boiling water drives a **generator** (say "jen-er-ay-tor").

❷ The generator pushes the powerful current along thick wires called cables. The cables are held high above the ground on pylons and carry the electricity to cities and towns.

Electricity flows along special pathways, called circuits (say "sur-kits"). Most circuits are made from metal wire because electricity flows through metal. Electricity doesn't flow through **materials** (say "ma-tir-ee-als"), such as plastic, rubber or wood. Electric wires are covered in plastic or rubber to make them safe to use. When electricity is moving, we call it an electric current.

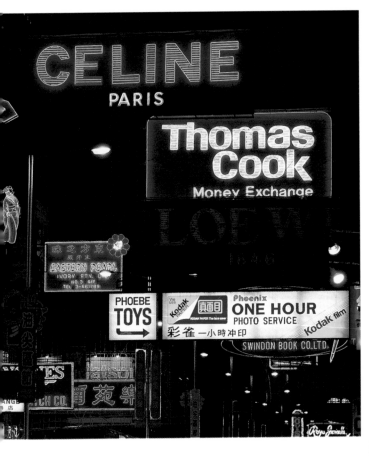

◄ Electricity allows stores to stay open all night.

Electricity from other sources

Not all power stations burn gas, coal or oil. Electricity can also be produced from **nuclear energy** or natural energy such as the Sun's heat, water or the wind. Natural forces never run out and do not harm the **environment**.

❸ In cities and towns, the current is divided into smaller currents which travel along thick underground cables to each street. Other cables branch off these to carry the current into people's homes.

▲ Wind generators use the force of the wind to make electricity.

ELECTRICITY IS DANGEROUS
ELECTRICITY WILL FLOW THROUGH YOUR BODY. IF YOU TOUCH A BARE WIRE OR A SOCKET THAT HAS ELECTRICITY FLOWING THROUGH IT, YOU WILL GET AN ELECTRIC SHOCK. THIS COULD KILL YOU.

Factory

A factory is a building where things are made. Most of the things we buy, such as cars, clothes and washing **machines**, are made in large numbers in factories. Factories can buy huge amounts of the **materials** (say "ma-tir-ee-als") they need, at the lowest possible prices. They use machines, which are operated by people or robots, to make the goods. **Mass production** is the cheapest way of making goods. That is why few things are made by hand today.

Inside a bike factory

1 Metal tubing for the bike frame is delivered to the factory.

6 Machines clean and paint the frames.

7 Some tricky parts of the bike frame are made by hand.

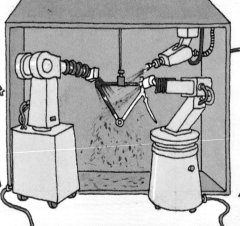

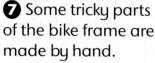

8 The small parts of the bike, such as brakes and gears, are stored in one part of the factory.

9 The small parts are fitted to the bike one at a time.

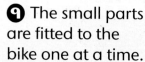

2 Sawing machines cut the tubing into different lengths.

3 Wire brushes rub the ends of the tubing smooth.

5 Robots join the tubing together to make the bike frame.

4 Other machines shape the tubing.

11 The wheels and seat are added to the bike.

10 The wheel spokes and tyres are fitted to the wheels.

12 The bike is taken to the **distribution warehouse**.

Fire

Fire is the hot, bright flame that is made when something burns. It gives off both heat and light, as well as smoke. If you have sat by a camp fire, you know how bright and warm a fire can be. People discovered fire nearly two million years ago. They found that if they hit two pieces of hard flint stone together, they could make a spark. If the spark landed on dry grass, it started a fire. To keep the fire burning, they needed **fuel** (say "fyoo-el") such as wood or coal, and air.

▲ When air is heated by fire, it rises. This is how a hot-air balloon works.

Fire for cooking

Controlled fire is very useful. People have learned to use fire for heating and cooking food. A gentle flame can make soup warm. A hot oven cooks a lump of soft dough so it becomes a crunchy biscuit.

Fire in factories

Fire is used in factories to make many kinds of things. The fire of a hot furnace melts metal so that it can be hammered into different shapes. A kiln is a kind of oven that uses fire to bake clay pots, or bricks, to make them hard.

▲ When a firework is lit, it becomes nearly 40 times as hot as the steam from a boiling kettle.

Emergency!
Fires can also be very dangerous.
Every town and city has a department
of people who are trained to fight fires.
Firefighters wear special equipment to
protect them from the smoke and flames.
They wear masks to keep their lungs
from filling with smoke. Without the
masks, they would suffocate.

Guitar

A guitar is a stringed musical instrument. Its body is made of light wood, such as pine, redwood or walnut. It is hollow inside and has a sound hole, and a long, thin neck. Usually, six strings made of nylon or steel, are stretched along the length of a guitar. They can be made tighter or looser by turning pegs at the top of the neck. Sounds are made by plucking or strumming the strings.

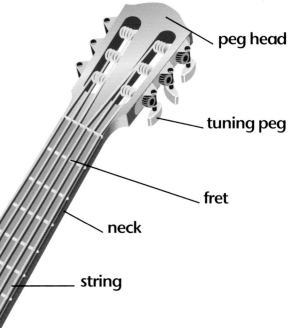

peg head

tuning peg

fret

neck

string

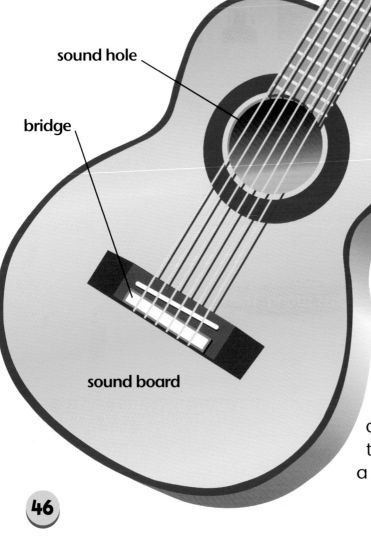

finger board

sound hole

bridge

sound board

Sound from string

❶ If you pluck a guitar string, it **vibrates** (say "vy-brayts") very quickly.

❷ The vibrating string shakes the air around it. The shaking reaches your ears as a sound.

❸ The hollow body of the guitar vibrates with the string and makes the sound louder.

❹ Pressing down on a string while you pluck it makes the sound higher, because the string is shorter.

Electric guitars

Electric guitars are **solid** and do not have a sound hole. When you pluck the strings, you send electrical signals to an amplifier (say "amp-liff-eye-er") to make the signals louder. Then the signals go to a speaker that changes them into sounds.

▲ An electric guitar can be louder than an ordinary guitar, and produces a greater number of different sounds.

now picture this

The largest guitar in the world was made in Indiana in 1991. The guitar is over 11 metres long (nearly as long as two limousines) and needs six people to play it.

See also Building, Fire, Store; ALL ABOUT PEOPLE Eating

Kitchen

▼ The chef, or cook, in a large restaurant uses a lot of equipment.

A kitchen is a room where people store and cook food, wash dirty dishes and keep all kinds of cooking and eating equipment, such as pots, pans, knives, bowls and plates.

Did you know?

Food was first stored in airtight tins in 1810, but the first tin-opener was not invented until 40 years later.

In the Food Museum in Switzerland, there is a small honey and sesame (say "sess-a-mee") cake that is thought to be nearly 4,200 years old. It was sealed in an airtight container inside an ancient Egyptian tomb.

Storing food

Fresh food does not last for more than a few days. After a week or two in the air, a fresh red apple turns brown and starts to rot.

Dried foods, such as raisins, stay fresh for months. In space, astronauts use food that is dried as a powder. They add water to their food in order to eat it.

 Food that is sealed inside an airtight tin lasts for several years.

Food spoils quickest when it is warm. Keeping food cold in a refrigerator helps it to last a few days longer.

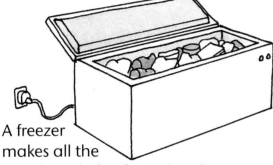

A freezer makes all the liquid inside food turn into ice. Frozen food lasts for up to one year.

Keeping clean
It is very important to keep a kitchen or cooking area clean. Cleaning kills **germs** that live and grow in dirty places. Be sure you wash your hands and your food before you start cooking.

▶ Not everyone uses a kitchen. In many countries, people live in small homes and cook their food outside.

 49

Light

Light is a kind of **energy** that we use in order to see. Stars and lamps make light, but the brightest light on Earth comes from the Sun. Sunlight comes to the Earth all the time, even when the sky is cloudy. Without light, the Earth would be pitch black, and nothing would be able to live and grow here. People once used candles or lanterns to provide light at night, but now we use electric light. The energy for electric lights is delivered through wires or by batteries.

▼ Sunlight seems to have no colour, but when it shines through rain drops, the colours mixed together in sunlight are split into a rainbow.

NEVER LOOK STRAIGHT AT THE SUN, EVEN WITH SUNGLASSES ON. IT IS SO BRIGHT THAT IT COULD DAMAGE YOUR EYES.

▶ At night, runways and aeroplanes are lit up with electric lights to make flying as safe as possible.

Light at night

At night, as our part of the Earth turns away from the Sun, we lose its light. We switch on lights that are powered by electricity and carry on our work or play.

▼ Light from a **laser beam** is so **powerful** that it can be used to drill a hole through strong metal.

Making a shadow

Rays of light will shine through something clear, like glass, but when light hits something that isn't clear, such as your body, it can't shine through.

Your body blocks out the light and leaves a patch behind you where there is no light. This patch is called a shadow.

Metal

A metal is a **material** (say "ma-tir-ee-al") that is often hard and shiny, and can be bent into different shapes. Iron, steel, copper and tin are all metals. Most metals are found in the earth. Some metals, such as iron, are found as rocks called ores. The ore has to be crushed and heated to get the metal out. Gold and silver are sometimes dug out of the ground and sometimes found as ores.

▼ Gold can sometimes be found in rivers and streams. "Panning" is a way of separating gold from other metals.

▲ A lump of gold dug out of the ground is called a nugget.

Melting metals

When metals are heated, they soften and can be pressed into different shapes. Metals harden again as they grow cool.

◄ This metal worker is using a hot flame to weld, or join, pieces of metal together.

If metals are heated to very high **temperatures**, they melt into a liquid and can be mixed together like paints. Iron will mix with tiny amounts of other metals to make steel, one of the strongest building materials in the world. Steel is more useful than the metals it comes from.

▶ Sometimes metals are melted down and poured into special moulds called bars, or ingots. It is easier to store metals like this.

World champion metal

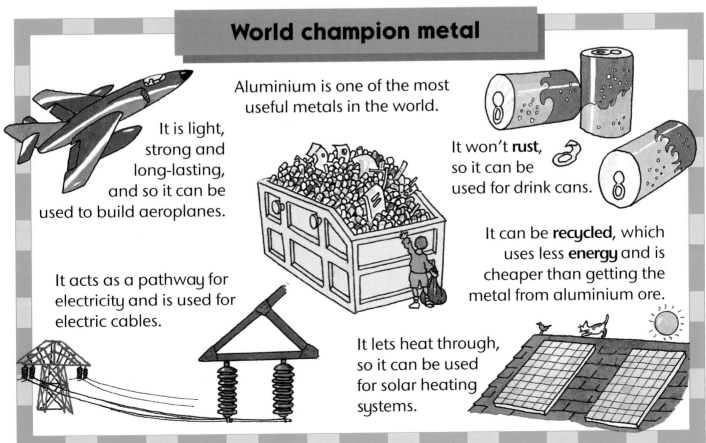

Aluminium is one of the most useful metals in the world.

It is light, strong and long-lasting, and so it can be used to build aeroplanes.

It won't **rust**, so it can be used for drink cans.

It can be **recycled**, which uses less **energy** and is cheaper than getting the metal from aluminium ore.

It acts as a pathway for electricity and is used for electric cables.

It lets heat through, so it can be used for solar heating systems.

Money

People use money to pay for the things they buy. Everyone needs some money to pay for services, such as heating and water, and to buy goods, such as food and clothes. Most people have to earn money by doing a job. For this, they are paid a **salary**.

Around the world

Every country in the world has its own kind of money, called currency (say "cur-en-see"). Pounds, dollars and yen are all currencies. When you visit another country, you usually have to change your money into the currency of that country before you can buy food or other goods from shops.

Did you know?

In Britain, cheques do not have to be written on paper. A man once wrote a cheque on the side of a cow, and the money was still paid out of his bank account.

In 1986 a Swiss bank brought out a machine that allowed wealthy customers to take out solid gold bars or gold coins from the bank vaults while the bank was closed.

Plastic cards

Many people use a plastic credit card to buy goods. Each card has a number written in code on a metal strip on the back. A **machine** at a checkout "reads" this number and links up with a computer at the customer's bank. The bank sends out a bill every month for the customer to pay.

▲ In most countries, people use money to buy the things they need.

now picture this

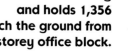

The world's largest credit card wallet is 75 metres long and holds 1,356 cards. It would reach the ground from the top of a 30-storey office block.

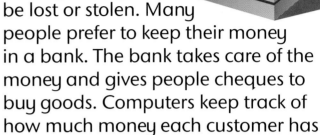

The history of money

Before there was any money, people exchanged one kind of goods for another. The first things used as money were shells, beans and beads.

The first coins were made of gold or silver, so that the coins themselves were valuable.

Today, paper money and coins are not made of valuable **materials** (say "ma-tir-ee-als"), but they are still worth the amount which they have stamped or printed on them.

In the bank

Carrying money about or storing it in a box can be risky. It may be lost or stolen. Many people prefer to keep their money in a bank. The bank takes care of the money and gives people cheques to buy goods. Computers keep track of how much money each customer has in the bank.

▲ Most banks have a safe made of strong steel where people's money can be kept secure.

Movie

A movie tells a story through sound and moving pictures. We can watch movies on a big screen in a cinema or on television. Movies usually begin as a script in which a writer tells a story. Then actors are chosen to play each character. Movies can be very exciting. Special effects can make you believe that animals talk, or that people can make friends with beings from outer space.

Did you know?

Walt Disney's famous mouse was first called Mortimer. He was renamed Mickey in 1928.

Hollywood's important Oscar awards are not just given to adults. In 1994, at the age of 11, Anna Paquin won an Oscar for her part in the film *The Piano*.

One hour of a movie uses up around 1,225 metres of film.

Making a movie

Movies are made by film companies. They often cost a lot of money. A film company hires hundreds of people who work together to make the movie.

❸ Much of the movie is made in a **studio**. Painters and set builders can make a studio look like the planet Mars or a street in the Wild West.

❶ The director is in charge of the filming. He or she decides how every part of the movie should look, and how the actors should perform.

❷ Actors learn the words of the script, and rehearse their parts before filming begins.

Cartoons

Cartoons are made by filming millions of drawings for a split second each.

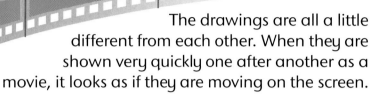

The drawings are all a little different from each other. When they are shown very quickly one after another as a movie, it looks as if they are moving on the screen.

❹ Sometimes stunt men and women perform dangerous stunts in the movie. They practise hard before filming begins.

❺ **Engineers** control the lighting on set, record the soundtrack and operate the cameras.

❻ After filming, the film editor takes the best parts and joins them together in a movie of the right length.

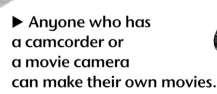

▶ Anyone who has a camcorder or a movie camera can make their own movies.

Museum

A museum is a building that displays interesting, unusual and often very old objects. Visitors come to the museum to see the objects, and learn from them. Most museums collect objects of a certain kind, such as paintings, spacecraft or things from other **cultures**. Some even collect toys.

Inside a museum

Some displays let people find out what it is like to do a job, for example to drive a train or fly a spacecraft.

Some visitors hire a guidebook and a tape that tell them about the displays.

There is often a store that sells books and pictures, or models, of the displays.

Museum guides show visitors around the displays.

Visitors pay to enter the museum.

Some museums have rooms where younger visitors can make models of the things on display in different parts of the museum.

Most museums have a café where visitors can eat and drink.

The museum has offices where the people who run the museum work.

All museums have an area where objects are cleaned and repaired.

Sometimes a museum puts on a special exhibition of objects not usually on display.

Some museums have exciting displays that visitors can make work for themselves.

In the museum library, people can look up information about different objects or people.

Curators are experts. They give talks about their displays, buy new objects, and arrange new displays for them.

59

See also Computer, Museum, Store, Telephone

Office

An office is a place where people plan, organize and carry out their work. It is like a control centre. Modern offices usually have lots of **machines** that make this work easier. All businesses have an office, as well as hospitals, shops and factories. Schools have offices too, where the school secretary works. She or he greets visitors to the school, makes the head teacher's telephone calls and types letters to parents and staff.

Important information, for example about students and staff, is kept in a filing cabinet and on computer.

A school office

A word processor is a computer that lets you type and correct letters on a screen before printing them out.

A calculator helps do sums quickly.

A telephone allows people in different places to talk to each other. If a student becomes ill, the secretary may call his or her family.

Photocopiers can copy letters in seconds. They can make 100 copies in less than one minute.

A fax machine can copy a sheet of paper, such as an order for more text books, and send it by telephone line to another fax machine in seconds.

An answering machine uses a tape to record messages from people who phone the office when no one is there.

61

Oil

Oil is a dark, thick liquid which lies deep inside the Earth. It was formed from tiny plants and animals that once lived in the sea. As they died, they sank to the bottom and were buried in mud. Over the years, the mud changed into hard, heavy rock.

The rock slowly pushed down on the rotting plants and animals, and changed them into the black, sticky **material** (say "ma-tir-ee-al") which we call oil. Finding oil and getting it out of the ground is hard work and expensive. It's worth the effort because oil is so useful.

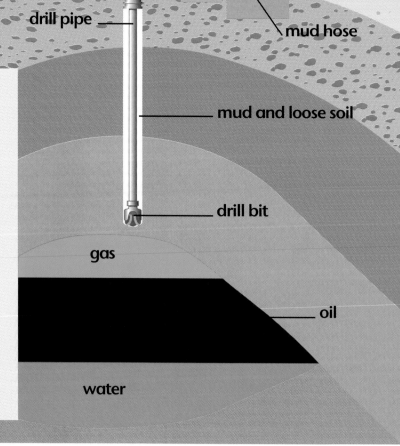

derrick

drill pipe

mud hose

mud and loose soil

drill bit

gas

oil

water

An oil well

Oil collects in holes inside rocks deep down in the Earth. Oil companies drill a well down to the oil. To keep the bit cool as they drill, they pump mud down inside the drill pipe. The mud flows back up to the surface outside the drill pipe and takes loose soil with it. When the drill strikes oil, the well is lined with a steel pipe. Oil flows to the surface along tubes inside the pipe.

At the refinery

When oil reaches the surface, it is piped to a factory called an oil refinery. Here it is heated until it separates into different kinds of oil. Light oils are used as **fuel** (say "fyoo-el") for **vehicles** (say "vee-ick-els") and electricity **generators** (say "jen-er-ay-tors"). Thicker oils are used for lubrication. Some oils are used to make other things such as plastic and nylon.

▶ Life on an oil rig at sea is dangerous and hard. The rig is so far from land that the workers are flown in by helicopter.

How is oil used?

Oil is used to make electricity. It is burned to heat water into the steam that drives the electricity generator.

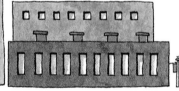

Oil is used to make nylon and other clothes fabrics.

Oil is used for fuels such as petrol and **diesel** (say "dee-zel"). Oil is also used to make different parts of a **machine** move against each other smoothly.

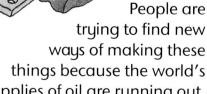

Tar that is used to cover roads is made from oil.

Oil is used in plastic and polythene (say "pol-ee-theen").

People are trying to find new ways of making these things because the world's supplies of oil are running out.

Plastic

Plastic is a factory-made **material** (say "ma-tir-ee-al") that can be moulded into different shapes. It was first made in the USA about 90 years ago. Plastic is light but strong, and can be very colourful. It is useful because it doesn't fall apart easily, or **rust** in the open air. Often plastic is used to make things that used to be made from natural materials, such as wood or metal.

▶ Plastic is stored as grains. The grains are melted down later on and poured into moulds.

How is plastic used?

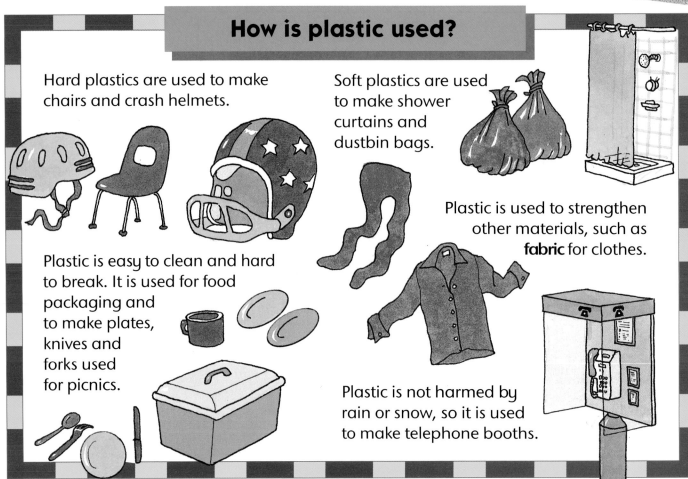

Hard plastics are used to make chairs and crash helmets.

Soft plastics are used to make shower curtains and dustbin bags.

Plastic is easy to clean and hard to break. It is used for food packaging and to make plates, knives and forks used for picnics.

Plastic is used to strengthen other materials, such as **fabric** for clothes.

Plastic is not harmed by rain or snow, so it is used to make telephone booths.

Recycling plastic

Plastic is made from oil, which is very valuable. The Earth's oil is being used up faster than fresh oil is being formed. One way of saving oil is to **recycle** plastic. Some places have recycling centres where different plastics are sorted. The plastics are taken to a factory where they are melted down and made into new things such as flower pots, traffic cones and dustbins.

▶ Before recycling, plastic objects must be sorted into soft and hard plastics. Different kinds of plastic are recycled in different ways.

Did you know?

The black lining inside a nonstick saucepan is a kind of plastic.

Perspex is a strong, clear plastic. It is used to build see-through squash courts for squash matches, so that as many people as possible can watch.

Plastic surgeons are named after the flexible or "plastic" skin that they mould.

Plastic in surgery

Some kinds of plastic are safe to use inside the human body. When people break their bones in an accident, the broken bones may be joined together again by plastic screws and pins. Surgeons use different plastics for the thread they use to sew up wounds, and to replace damaged parts of organs such as the heart.

Radio

A radio is a **machine** that sends out and receives electrical signals along radio waves. Most people use radios to listen to music, news, and other programmes **broadcast** from a radio station. Two-way radios allow people in different places to talk directly to each other. Two-way radios are often used by the armed forces, as well as by train, bus and taxi companies, to keep people in touch with each other.

▲ Sports commentators use a radio headset to keep in touch with the people at the television studio.

A radio broadcast

Radios send out messages by using invisible signals called radio waves. The signals are silent until they reach another radio which can turn them into sounds.

❶ At a radio station, newsreaders and disc jockeys sit in a **studio** to broadcast their programme. As they speak, their voices create **vibrations** (say "vy-bray-shuns") in the air. The microphone changes the vibrations into electrical signals.

❷ The electrical signals travel along a wire to a transmitter.

3 The transmitter changes the electrical signals into radio waves. The waves travel through the air, hundreds of miles away from the transmitter.

4 In less than a second, the waves reach your radio **aerial** (say "air-ee-al"), which changes the waves back into electrical signals.

5 The signals pass down the aerial to your radio. Inside your radio the speaker turns the signals back into sounds that your ears can hear.

Keeping in touch

Radio waves can be used to keep ships at sea in contact with their port, and astronauts in space in touch with the Earth. Radios help to keep people safe. Police officers carry radios with them to talk to the police station or call other officers for help.

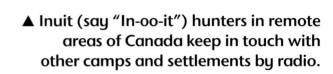

▲ Inuit (say "In-oo-it") hunters in remote areas of Canada keep in touch with other camps and settlements by radio.

◀ If an athlete is injured, medical staff can radio quickly for a stretcher or ambulance.

Robot

A robot is a **machine** that can be used instead of a person to do a job. Most robots are controlled by computers. Many robots are moving arms that do not have bodies. They are often used in factories to make **mass-produced** goods. Robots are also used for dangerous jobs. If the police find a bomb, a robot may be used to defuse it.

Building cars

Robots are used to do the simple jobs needed to build cars. The cars move along a track between the robots as they work.

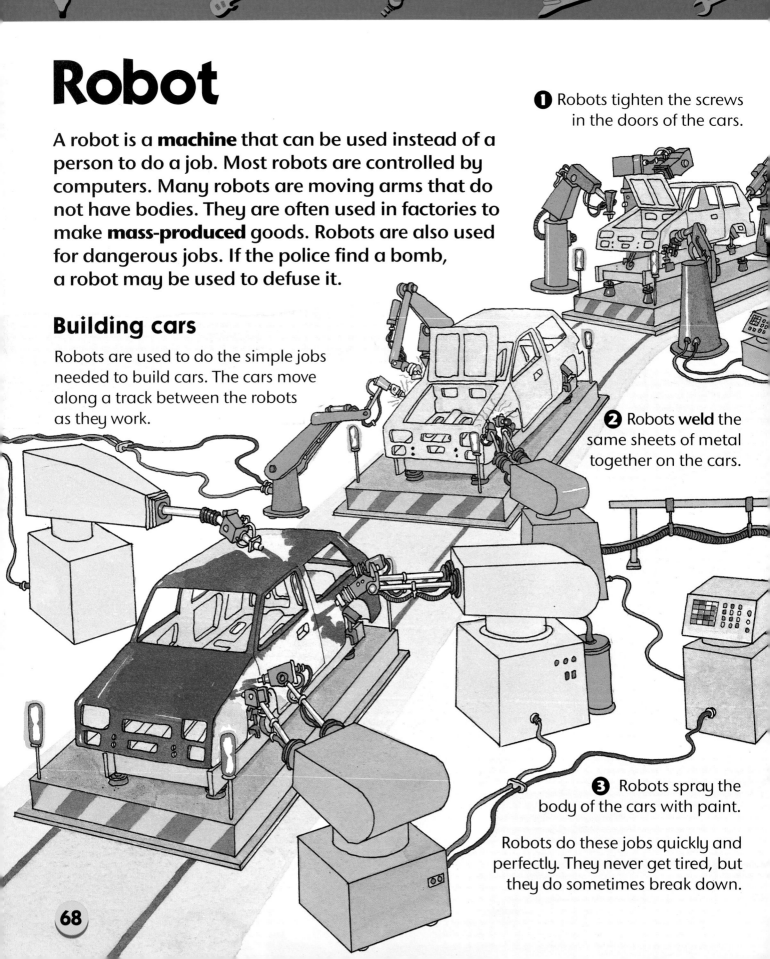

❶ Robots tighten the screws in the doors of the cars.

❷ Robots **weld** the same sheets of metal together on the cars.

❸ Robots spray the body of the cars with paint.

Robots do these jobs quickly and perfectly. They never get tired, but they do sometimes break down.

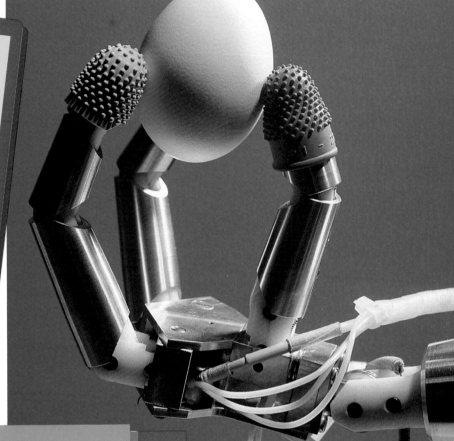

Did you know?

A robot sheep-shearer has been invented in Australia. The robot can shear a sheep in just 100 seconds, more than one minute faster than a human shearer can.

In Japan, some places do not have enough Shinto priests for all the **shrines**. Some shrines are now using robots to chant prayers instead of priests.

▶ Some robots have to hold small or delicate objects. This robot "hand" is being tested for its grip.

Under the sea

In 1986, divers used a robot called Jason Junior to explore the wreck of the ocean liner *Titanic*. The wreck lay on the sea bed four kilometres below the surface of the sea.

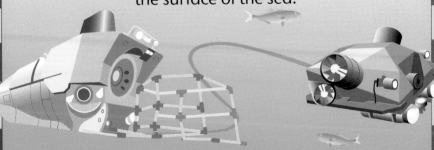

Jason Junior carried two cameras that took pictures of the *Titanic*. Jason Junior was attached by a cable to a submarine, and the submarine's crew controlled it from there by computer.

▲ This robot helps to raise money for the Leslie Frost Natural Resources Centre in Ontario, Canada.

Roller coaster

A roller coaster is a ride at a fairground. It is made up of cars that run freely along a track. The track goes up and down, and around sharp bends. Sometimes it loops the loop. A roller coaster has no engine. Instead, invisible **forces** make it speed up and slow down.

Gravity

There is a force called **gravity** that tugs everything towards the middle of the Earth. Gravity that makes something you have dropped fall to the ground. You cannot feel gravity, but it also keeps you on the surface of the Earth, no matter where in the world you are.

Into action

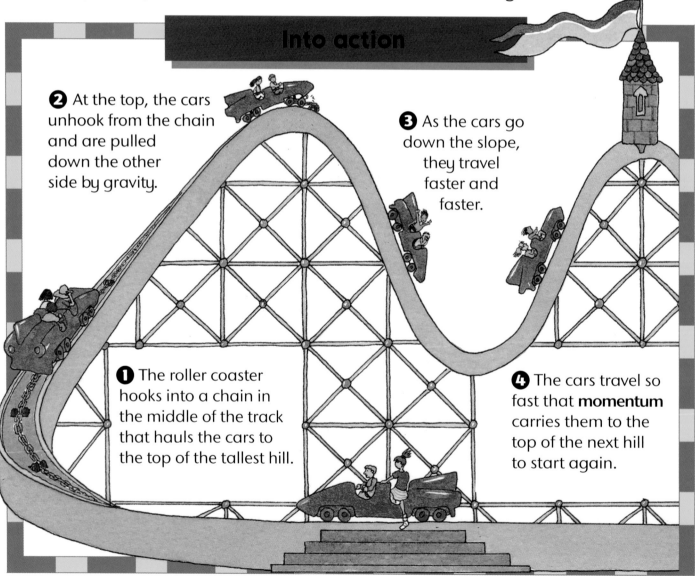

2 At the top, the cars unhook from the chain and are pulled down the other side by gravity.

3 As the cars go down the slope, they travel faster and faster.

1 The roller coaster hooks into a chain in the middle of the track that hauls the cars to the top of the tallest hill.

4 The cars travel so fast that **momentum** carries them to the top of the next hill to start again.

When a roller coaster loops the loop, the passengers feel pushed back into their seats. This is because momentum keeps their bodies travelling upwards for a short time as the cars start to come down.

▼ Even if a roller coaster in a loop had no outside wheels to grip the track, it would not fall off the track as long as it was travelling fast enough.

See also Roller coaster, Telephone, Television; A FIRST ATLAS The United States and Mexico;

Space shuttle

A space shuttle is a spacecraft that can fly into space again and again. It may take new **satellites** into space, or repair ones already there. Sometimes it carries astronauts who perform scientific experiments. The shuttle has two parts, one for the astronauts, and another made up of the booster rockets and **fuel** (say "fyoo-el") tank. Both parts of the shuttle can be reused. This makes the space shuttle different from spacecraft that can only make one flight.

❹ The shuttle's smaller engines guide it into **orbit**. **Gravity** keeps it circling the Earth until its mission is over.

❸ Nine minutes later the fuel tank is empty and drops away.

A shuttle mission

❶ On the launch pad, the shuttle's booster rockets fire and begin to burn fuel. The shuttle lifts off.

❷ Two minutes later, the boosters have run out of fuel. They fall into the sea.

The boosters are fished out of the sea to be used again.

5 When it has finished its mission, the shuttle's engines slow the shuttle down and steer it back towards the Earth.

6 The shuttle is pulled down faster towards the Earth by gravity.

7 The shuttle enters the Earth's **atmosphere** (say "at-moss-fear"). As it pushes through the air, **friction** (say "frick-shun") makes the shuttle heat up and glow red-hot.

▲ Astronauts can be fixed to the robotic arm in the cargo bay to help them inspect the shuttle's cargo.

8 The shuttle glides down, without engine **power**, and lands on an ordinary runway.

Store

A store is a place where goods are sold. For example, a supermarket sells food and drinks. Some stores sell one kind of goods but big department stores sell many. Often stores are self-service. This means that you walk around the store, putting all the things you need in a shopping trolley. Before leaving, you pay for your goods at the checkout.

Inside a supermarket

In the office, people hire staff and pay them, take care of all the money, order new deliveries and make sure they arrive.

The in-store bakery makes fresh bread, cakes and pastries to sell in the supermarket.

Goods are stored in the stockroom.

Assistants have a break in the staff room.

Trucks bring goods to the store. The drivers park in the delivery area to unload.

Video cameras film people shopping. They help security guards to catch shoplifters.

Assistants at the deli counter serve customers with fresh cheeses, cold meats and salads.

The manager is the person in charge of the store.

Some assistants fill the shelves with goods from the stockroom.

At the checkout, the bar codes, or black lines that record the price of each item, are "read" by a **laser beam**. The cash register adds up all the prices, tells the cashier how much change to give the customer, and prints a receipt (say "re-seet").

Automatic doors open when people walk on a special mat in front of the door. They close behind people when they leave.

Most supermarkets have a car park so that customers can wheel their groceries straight to the car.

Telephone

A telephone is a **machine** that is used to talk to people in another place. The sound of your voice doesn't travel very far on its own. Telephones use electricity to change your voice into signals that flash along electrical cables or cables made of **optical fibre**. The signals can reach a telephone in another street or another country in just a few seconds. Cordless telephones act like two-way radios. They change your voice into radio waves that travel to another telephone through the air.

A long-distance call

1 As you press the numbers on your telephone, they are changed into electrical signals.

3 The telephone exchange changes the light signals into radio waves. The waves are beamed into space by a transmitter.

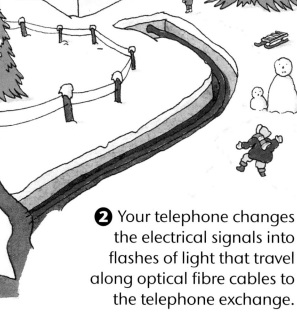

2 Your telephone changes the electrical signals into flashes of light that travel along optical fibre cables to the telephone exchange.

4 A **satellite** in space receives the waves and beams them back to a telephone exchange in another country.

5 Your friend's telephone receives the waves from the telephone exchange and rings.

6 When your friend speaks, his or her voice is changed into signals which travel back along the same route to your telephone.

Optical fibre

Inside an optical fibre, light flashes backwards and forwards across the fibre. This allows signals to travel round bends. Modern telephones use optical fibres because light travels faster than electricity and the fibres carry more signals than electrical wires can.

light

▲ Optical fibres inside a cable are made of glass or plastic and are the width of a human hair.

Television

A television is a **machine** that uses radio waves to make moving pictures appear on a screen in the television set, while sounds come from the speaker. Many people in the world have a television in their home. Others have more than one. Some people watch only the news. Others watch television all day. Today, television is one of the most important ways people learn about what is happening in the world.

A television broadcast

Around the world

Television companies use space **satellites** to send their programmes around the world. They send radio waves up to a satellite, which then beams them down to receivers on the ground. This allows people to sit in comfort at home and watch an event that is being **broadcast** from another country, for example the Olympic Games, as it is taking place.

❶ At the television studio, cameras change the images they "see" into electrical picture signals. Microphones change sound **vibrations** (say "vy-bray-shuns") into electrical sound signals.

❷ The picture and sound signals travel along wires to a transmitter. The transmitter changes the signals into radio waves and sends them through the air.

Video recording

Once radio waves have been changed into electrical signals, they can be saved as patterns on magnetic video tape. This allows people to record programmes and play them back through their television sets whenever they want.

▶ Some camera operators use a monitor screen to see which camera's signals are being broadcast.

❺ The sound signals travel to the speaker where they are changed back into sounds.

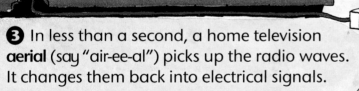

❸ In less than a second, a home television **aerial** (say "air-ee-al") picks up the radio waves. It changes them back into electrical signals.

❹ The signals flow along wires into the television set. The picture signals are used to light up dots on the television screen to make the colour pictures.

Tractor

A tractor is a **vehicle** (say "vee-ick-el") with large wheels, and a **powerful diesel** (say "dee-zel") engine. Tractors were invented about 100 years ago. They pull heavy **machines** on farms, such as ploughs and seed drills. Tractors work faster than animals and do not get tired. In one day a tractor can plough as many fields as a horse-drawn plough can work in one week.

Driving force

A tractor's engine is bigger and more powerful than a car's, but it is cheaper to run. Diesel oil costs less than petrol, and the engine needs less **fuel** (say "fyoo-el") to work.

The exhaust (say "ex-orst") pipe takes waste **fumes** out of the engine.

The brake drums slow the wheels down so that they stop.

The driver's cab is high up to give a good view.

The steering wheel changes the direction of the front wheels.

The engine burns fuel and gives the tractor the **power** to move.

The rear wheels give the tractor a good grip on muddy ground.

The gears give the wheels the right amount of power for the job they have to do.

A machine for all seasons

Farmers use tractors to pull different pieces of machinery at different times of the year:

In spring, a plough breaks up the soil for planting seeds. A seed drill puts the right amount of seed into the ploughed soil. It covers the seeds over so that birds don't eat them.

In summer, a sprayer soaks the growing crops with a spray that kills pests.

In the autumn, the tractor works alongside a combine harvester to gather in the harvested crops.

Getting a grip

Tractors have to work where there is a lot of mud. To stop them from getting stuck, the huge wheels on a tractor have thick tyres with a deep tread. The grooves in the tread let muddy water escape from under them, and help the tyre to grip the ground beneath.

The front wheels guide the tractor in the right direction.

▲ Oil makes the engine work smoothly by reducing **friction** (say "frick-shun").

Train

A train is a line of cars pulled by an engine along a railway track. Trains are used to transport goods and people. The first trains were invented about 150 years ago and were pulled by steam engines. Most modern trains run on **diesel** (say "dee-zel") oil or electricity.

▶ Trains can travel in all sorts of weather. In high-up places, snow ploughs fixed to the front of engines clear snow off the tracks.

A modern train

The front of the engine is rounded in shape so that it can push through the air more easily.

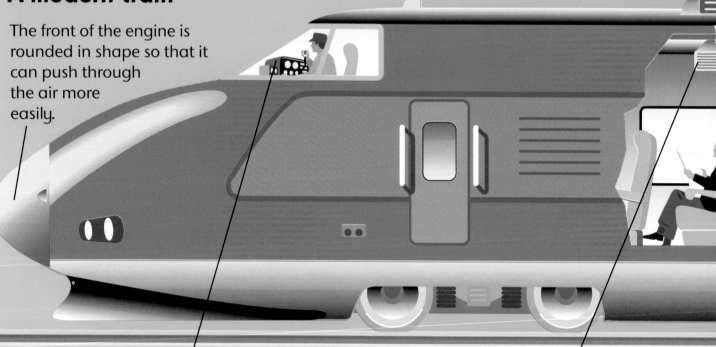

The driver's cab has an instrument panel and a radio. The radio allows the driver to talk to the signal operators who control all the trains on the line. If there is an accident further up the line, the signal operators can warn the driver to stop.

Air-conditioning keeps the cars cool in hot weather. A heating system keeps them warm when the weather is cold.

Trains and the environment

Trains may be the best form of transport in the future. A train can carry a heavier load than a truck or bus, and uses less **fuel** (say "fyoo-el"). This helps to keep the **environment** clean. Trains also keep heavy trucks off the roads, making them quieter and safer for other drivers to use.

▶ To make room for roads and walkways, some cities have railway tracks that go over head or run underground.

Modern electric trains often run on electricity that comes from cables overhead. Electric trains do not need a fuel tank, so they weigh less and travel faster than diesel trains.

Keeping track

Trains have smooth metal wheels that have a sloping edge. This shape keeps the wheels on the track around bends. A rim, or flange, on the inside of each wheel keeps them on the track around very tight bends.

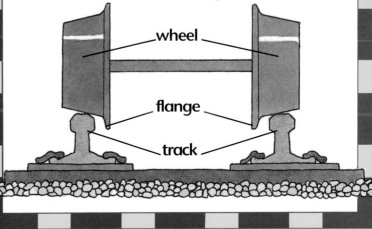

wheel

flange

track

83

Truck

A truck is a large, **powerful** road **vehicle** (say "vee-ick-el") that carries goods from one place to another. Trucks are designed (say "de-zyned") and built to do different jobs. The simplest kinds of truck take groceries to shops. A huge logging truck can load whole tree trunks on its trailer and take them from a forest to a timber yard.

▲ Dump trucks use an arm to tip up their trailer and unload their cargo.

A refrigerated truck

The air deflector helps air flow smoothly over the top of the truck so that it can go faster.

The cab is where the driver rides.

The truck's **diesel** (say "dee-zel") engine can pull heavy loads.

Double wheels spread the load over a wide surface, and keep the truck steady if a tyre punctures.

The **fuel** (say "fyoo-el") tank stores diesel oil.

▶ In Australia there are huge road trains. Each truck can pull up to three trailers at a time.

The refrigerated trailer keeps the load of food or drinks inside it fresh.

Working in pairs

Most big trucks are articulated (say "ar-tik-you-lay-ted"). This means they are built in two pieces. They have an engine in front and a trailer behind.

Being built like this lets the truck turn corners more tightly than it could if it were built in one piece.

85

Wheel

A wheel is a circle of strong **material** (say "ma-tir-ee-al") set around a centre axle (say "ax-el"). The wheel was invented about 5,000 years ago. People found it was much easier to carry goods in a cart with wheels than it was to drag them along the ground. The wheel is a simple but important invention that is used in almost all modern forms of transport.

Wheels for speed

At first wheels were **solid**, but solid wheels are often heavy and slow a **vehicle** (say "vee-ick-el") down. Wheels with spokes are light so that vehicles can gain speed more quickly.

Wheels at work

An object sliding along the ground rubs against the ground and is slowed down by **friction** (say "frick-shun").

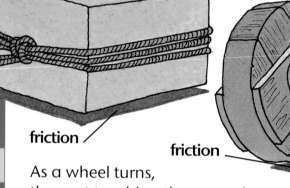

friction

friction

As a wheel turns, the part touching the ground is always changing. There is very little rubbing against the ground, and less friction.

▲ Motorbike wheels are light and can travel very fast.

▶ The Ferris wheel at a fairground is made with spokes so that it is strong, but light, and will not collapse.

Axles and bearings

To stop a wheel rubbing against its axle and being slowed down by friction, the axle is surrounded by a ring of shiny, metal bearings. Bearings can be shaped like balls, rollers or needles. As the wheel and axle turn, the bearings turn round, cutting down on friction.

Wheels on a Rollerblade

ball bearing

rubber tyre

axle

Glossary

Aerial Something that gives out or picks up radio waves that travel through the air.

Atmosphere The layer of air and other gases that surround the Earth.

Bound Something stuck or sewn together.

Broadcast Sent out by radio waves through the air.

Culture The ideas, crafts and customs of different countries or peoples.

Diesel A thick, heavy fuel made from oil.

Distribution warehouse The place where goods are kept before going to a shop.

Efficient Something that works without wasting too much energy.

Energy What makes people and machines able to do work. Energy comes from things such as fuels, the Sun, water or wind.

Engineer Someone who plans, builds or looks after things such as machines, engines, roads and bridges.

Environment The world around you.

Fabric Cloth used for making things such as clothes, and for covering furniture.

Fibreglass A material that is made of glass threads.

Filter A thing like a sieve that allows some materials through and keeps others out.

Force A push or pull that changes the way an object moves or starts it moving.

Friction The rubbing of things against each other that slows them down.

Fuel Something that gives out energy as heat or power when it burns.

Fumes Smoke, gas or vapour that is often irritating.

Generator A machine that changes energy from its moving parts into electrical energy.

Germ A tiny living thing that can make people and animals sick.

Gravity The force that pulls things into the centre of the Earth. Gravity also pulls the planets towards the Sun.

Laser beam A very narrow, powerful ray of light that can cut through hard materials.

Lens A curved piece of glass or plastic that bends light.

Machine Something with moving parts that work together to do a job.

Mass produce To make something in large numbers. This way of making things is called mass production.

Material The thing an object is made from.

Momentum The force that makes a moving object keep going in the same direction.

Negative A picture on photographic film that shows shadows as light areas and light areas as dark patches.

Optical fibre A thin thread of plastic or glass that lets rays of light travel along inside it.

Orbit The curved path of a planet, moon or spacecraft around a planet or star.

Power The strength to do a job.

Power station A large factory where generators make electricity.

Propeller Something that has blades fixed to a centre hub and moves a ship or airplane forwards when it turns.

Radar A way of tracking ships or airplanes by sending out radio waves. Waves that hit an object bounce back again.

Rays Light that is travelling in straight lines.

Recycle To use an object or material to make something else.

Rust When iron or steel turns brown and breaks up in damp air.

Salary Money paid to someone each month in return for work.

Satellite A thing that circles planets. People make machines called satellites in order to send signals from one country to another or to take photographs of the Earth.

Shrine A place where people pay respect to gods or saints.

Solid Something that is made in one piece and has a set shape and size.

Source A place where things come from.

Streamlined Something that is smooth and even so that it can move quickly without wasting much energy.

Studio A place where people make movies, records, or programs for radio or television.

Temperature A level of heat. Your temperature is how hot you are.

Tread The pattern of ridges on a tire that helps it grip wet or muddy ground.

Treatment plant A factory for cleaning water.

Vehicle A machine that is used to carry people or goods.

Vibrate To move backwards and forwards very fast. We call these movements **vibrations**.

Weld To join pieces of metal by melting and pressing them together so that they cool in one piece.

Index

A

aerial *67, 79*
aeroplane *12*-13, 51, 53
air-conditioning 82
air deflector 84
airport 13
aluminium 13, 19, 53
amplifier 46
Anna Paquin 56
answering machine 61
aperture 28
arched bridge 22
architect 24
articulated truck 85
artist 56
astronaut *67, 72*
atmosphere 73
Australia 69, 85
automatic door 26, 75
axle *86, 87*

B

bakery 74
ball bearing 87
bank 54, 55
bar code 75
basin 14
bath 14
bathroom 14-15, 25, 33
beam bridge *22*
bearing *87*
bike *16-17*, 18, *40-41*
boat *18*-19
Boeing 747 13
book 20-21, 58
booster rocket *72*
brake *17, 30, 40, 80*
brake drum 30, 80

brake pedal 30
brick 25
bricklayer 25
bridge *22*-23
Britain 54
broadcasting 66-67, 78-79
bubble bath 15
builder 24, 25
building 23, *24-25*
buildings *32-33, 40*, 58
bus *26-27, 33, 83*

C

cable *22, 24, 25, 27, 33, 38, 39, 53, 69, 76, 83*
café 59
calculator 9, *60*
camcorder 57
camera *28*-29, 57, *69, 78, 79*
Canada 67, 69
car 26, *30-31, 40, 68*
car ferry 18
car park 75
cargo 13, 73
carpenter 25
cartoon 56, *57*
cement 24, 25
cement mixer 25
chain 16
chef 48
cheque 54, 55
circuit 38
city *32-33*
clock *34-35*
clothing 40, *63*, 64
coin *55*
computer *21, 36-37*, 54, 55, 60, 69

computer scanner 36
concrete 23
cooking 42, 48, 49
copper 52
cordless telephone 76, *77*
credit card 54
curator 59

D

deli 75
delivery area 74
derrick 62
detergent 15
diesel oil *63, 80, 82, 84*
digital clock 34
director 56
disc jockey 66
disk drive 37
diving watch 34
drain 32
dried food 49
drill bit 62
drill pipe 62
drink can *53*
driver's cab 80, 82, 84
dump truck *24, 84*

E

Earth 50, 62, 70, 72, 73
egg timer *35*
electrical signal 66, 67, 76, 77, 78, 79
electrician 25
electricity 11, 24, 27, 31, 32, 33, 38-39, 46, 47, 50, 51, 53, 63, 66, 67, 76-77, 79, 82, 83
electricity generator 63

encyclopedia 21
energy 10, 11, 16, 19,
    30, 31, 38, 39, 50, 53
engine 12, 19, 26, 30, *54,*
    72, 73, *80,* 81, 82, *84*
engineer 13, 23, 31,
    37, 57
England 22
environment 17, 39, 83
exhaust *30,* 31, *80*

F

factory 9, *40-41,* 42, 44,
    60, 63, 65, 68
fax machine 61
Ferris wheel 87
fibreglass 19, 44
fiction section 21
filing cabinet 60
film *28,* 29, 56
film editor 57
filter 31
finger board 46
fire 42-43
firefighter 43
firework 42
flange 83
flint 42
floating 18, 19
floorboard 25
floppy disk 36, *37*
flower pot 65
flying 12
food 48, 49, 54, 74
Food Museum,
    Switzerland 48
food tins 48, 49
force 16, 70
foundation 24
freezer 49
fret 46

friction 73, *86,* 87
fuel 10, 12, 13, 19, 31, 38,
    42, 63, 72, 80, 82, 83
fuel tank *72,* 83, *84*
fumes 30, 31, 80

G

gas pipe 32
gear 16, 30, 40
generator 10, 38, 39, 63
germ 15, 49
glass 44-45, 77
gold 52, 54, 55
gravity 70, 72, 73
guidebook 58
guitar 46-47

H

handlebar 17
hard disk 37
head teacher 60
headlight 31
health 14
heat 38, 42, 52, 63
heating 54, 82
helicopter 63
Hollywood 56
hot-air balloon 42
hourglass *35*
house *24, 25*

I

ignition 30
indicator light 31
Inuit people 67
iron 45, 52

J

Japan 69
Jason Junior *69*
jet engine 12

K

keyboard 36, 37
kiln 42
kitchen *25,* 33, 48-49

L

lamp 50
laser beam *21,* 51, 75
launch pad 72
lead crystal 44
lens 28
library 21, *59*
light 38, 39, 42, 50-51,
    76, 77
lightning 38, 44
limestone 44
liquid 62
logging truck 84

M

machine 8-9, 10-11, 12,
    21, 28, 36, 38, 40-41, 45,
    63, 66, 68, 76, 78, 81
manager 75
mass production 40, 68
material 13, 19, 23, 38,
    40, 44, 52-53, 55, 62, 86
melting 53, 64, 65
metal 19, 52-53, 83
metal ore 52
Mickey Mouse 56
microphone *66,* 78
momentum 70, 71
money 54-55, 56
motorbike 86
mould *45,* 53, 64
mouse 37
movie *56-57*
movie camera 28, 29
mud 64, 80, 81

mud hose 62
museum 32, 33, *58-59*
music 46

N

negative 29
newsreader 66
nickel 44
nugget 52
nylon 63

O

oar *19*
off-road vehicle 31
office 59, *60-61*
oil 62-63, 81
oil refinery 63
oil rig 63
oil tanker *18*
Olympic Games 78
optical fibre 76, *77*
orbit 72
Oscar award 56

P

paper 20, 21, 55
peg head 46
personal computer 36
Perspex 65
petrol 30, 31, 63
photocopier 61
photograph 28-29
piping *14-15, 25,* 32, 33
plasterer 25
plastic 54, 63, 64-65, 77
plastic surgeon 65
plough 80, *81*
plumber 25
police 37, 67, 68
pollution 31
polythene 63

power 30, 73, 80
power station *38*, 39
printer 21, *37*
printing 20, 21
propeller 19
publisher 20
pumping station 14

R

radar 13
radio *27, 66-67*, 82
radio waves 66, 76, 78, 79
raft 18
railway 26, 82
rainbow 50
receipt 75
recycling 45, 53, 65
refrigerated food 49, 85
refrigerated truck *84-85*
restaurant 32
River Humber 22
road train 85
robot 40, 41, *68-69*, 73
robot hand 69
robotic arm 73
rock 52, 62
roller coaster *70*-71
Roman numerals 35
root bridge 23
rowing boat *19*
rubber tyre 87
runway 51, 73
rust 53, 64

S

safety rules 16, 39, 43, 45,
    50, 83
sailing boat *19*
salary 54

sand 44
satellite 72, 73, *76, 77*, 78
saucepan 65
scaffolding 25
school office *60-61*
screen 36
script 56
secretary *60*
security guard 75
seed drill *80*
sewer 14, 32
shadow 51
shampoo 15
ship *18*, 19, 67
signal operator 82
silver 52, 55
skyscraper 24
snow plough 82
soap 15
solar heating system *53*
solar-powered car 31
sound 46, 56, 57, 78, 79
sound board 46
sound hole 46
space shuttle *72-73*
speaker *67*, 78, 79
spoke *16*, 41, 86, 87
star 50
"Stealth" bomber 13
steel 19, 23, 52, 53, 55
steering wheel 30, 80
stockroom 74
storage tower 14
store 32, 60, *74-75*, 84
storybook 20, 21
streamlining 12, 31
studio *56, 78*
stunt 57
submarine 69
suburb 33

subway *33*
Sun 39, 50
sunlight 50
supermarket *74-75*
suspension bridge *22*

T

tap *14*, 33
tar *63*
telephone 33, 60, *76-77*
telephone exchange 76, 77
television 56, *78-79*
theatre 33
ticket machine 27
time 34, 35
time zone 34
timetable 27
tin 52
Titanic 69
toilet 14, 33
track *70*, 82, *83*
tractor *80*-81
train *82-83*
tram 27, 33
transmitter 67, *76, 78*
transport 12-13, 16-17,
    18-19, 26-27, 30-31, 72-73,
    82-83, 84-85, 86-87
tread *17*, 81
treatment plant *14, 15*
tripod 28
truck 18, *54-55*, 74, 85
tuning peg 46
two-way radio 66
typing 36, 60
tyre 17, 31, 80, 81

U

underground 26, *32*, 83
underwater camera 29

V

vehicle 12-13, 16-17, 18-19,
    22, 26-27, 30-31, 63, 72-73,
    80-81, 84-85, 86
viaduct *22*
vibrations 48, 66, 78
video camera 28
video recording 79
viewfinder 28

W

Walt Disney 56
water 14-15, 33
water pipe 14, 33
welding 68
wheel *41, 80, 81,*
    83, 84, 86-*87*
wire 50
word processor 60
work 8, 9, 10, 11,
    54, 60